A Season of Seasons

Discovering God Within Every Storm

By

Breana Smith

A Season of Seasons

Discovering God Within Every Storm

Copyright 2021 by Breana Smith

Dedication

For this book I give honor to my Lord and
Savior Jesus Christ who helped me to
eventually win every battle I faced. And to
everyone who's been through hard times but
chose courage and kept on living.

Introduction

Here's the truth.

Nobody really knows what it's like to walk in your shoes. People are quick to judge, while others believe they have all the answers. Our loved ones sometimes put pressure on us without even knowing it, and regardless of their good intentions, we still bleed on the inside.

At times we suffer either because we didn't do right by others or because we didn't do right by our own selves. Maybe we didn't listen, or maybe we refused to learn. Life can really suck. But what I've learned is that even the most pain can eventually produce great joy. Even the tallest tree started out small but grew because of sunshine and rain.

We should embrace both the happiness and the pain. Our dark times can be so uncomfortable and cold, and we all desire the sun to shine on our faces again. For me, the sun is Jesus Christ. He taught me through all my struggles that He is the one who can make anything beautiful.

Jesus' love opened my own heart and taught me that even the worst parts of me could transform into the best parts of me. He helped me to keep going, even though I gave up many times. I once convinced myself that because of my bad decisions I was disqualified from being loved unconditionally. The journey of finally loving myself showed me how wrong I was. But I've learned that there is a set time for everything.

My pain once felt like it was never going to end, but I kept growing and changing until it eventually did. It's been a long time coming, but everything happens for a reason. Just as night turns to day, and winter into spring, change creates a new season.

My Star

You were my star

Shinning so bright when you smile

Eyes lighting up, twinkling

Heart so full, or so I thought

I carry you with me everywhere

We breathe the same air

My fingers through your curly hair

Kiss as soft as rose petals on my skin

So excited to let you in

I love to love you

I love being in love, but not when you hurt me

I don't like hurting you

I try to get through

You were my star

I can't see anyone except you

My whole world is black because you blinded me

Being who you are, tainted

You were my star

Desperation

You needed me

I need you

Nothing else gets me through

Good for a while

Happy for a time

Life without you should be a crime

Come into me and stay

Seep out of me, go away

I don't need this love

But I need this love

It's never enough for me

And I'll never give it up

I'm crazy for you

Sacrifice my life and then pray for you

I'm not okay with you

The things you use to do

I see you're better now

Ready for the next girl

But I need you too

You are my world

Can you deal with both of us?

Cause' I'm not leaving

She's always on your mind, I'm there too

I won't stay

I'm wishing these scars would go away

I'm getting better too

Cuddling with my next dude

But it'll always be you, the one I run to

Your intoxicating love invigorates me

I'm desperate

Like It Never Happened

All those words you said

Are running through my head

Thinking like it was yesterday

Please fade away

Trying to undo your wrongs

But still singing the same song

Is it possible to let you in again?

To pretend like it never happened

Have you ever

Had that one special person

Do you wrong

Never thinking that they would hurt you

Feelings cut to your core

It was worse than a sore

Trying to move on, but you still love them

Ever love somebody with all that you have

And then they start running to you

Back from the past

Saying "hey, I'm sorry, let's do it all again, but let's
start as friends"
You're trying your best to pull yourself together
But this person coming back is bringing stormy
weather
You know you want to, but then again you don't
Who says you won't?
Wanna get back
To those special times, late, night, phone, talking
It wasn't bad, holding hands while you're walking
Thinking this person is your everything
Worth more than diamond rings
Until they sing
The song of pain that still remains
Seeing their face reminds you of everything
Taking a big risk with your heart such as this
But when you're without them, you suffer from the
miss
Sitting down asking God what should you do
You need guidance from above cause you don't
want to lose
And if I do it all again, I think I might end up dead
Because of all those words you said

It made me lose my head

I had spent so much bread

Now I'm laying in my bed

No plan to get ahead

Yeah, you heard what I said

But please, leave me be so I can heal from things I

dread

Word

Peaceful Mind

Peaceful mind, never am I

Clouds are never still

Forever is the sky

I took my time

Wasted on you

Worried of your thoughts of me

That had me so blue

I was nothing

You were everything

The beginning created an end to my sanity

Who are we?

Not who we use to be

Lies became reality

Nothing was ever stable

Not even with time

Peaceful mind, never am I

Halfway There

One silent night
One silent fight
Only one right
Cuddle me so tight
Head space so high
You made love to me a second time
Tried my best to be fine
Thoughts lost all night
You saw I wasn't myself
Took my flower anyway
Tears at the end of the day
Your love is never ever fair
I was only halfway there

Control

Trapped breath
Forever gasping for air
What have you done to me?
This isn't fair
Everywhere I go, you're there
Feeling you through the strands of my hair
Hoping to not see you
But expecting to see you
Anxiety creeping on me
You broke me, can't you see
My thoughts end with you
What can I do to please you?
Fake love is so old
Why am I under your control

Sorry

I'm sorry if this hurts you baby

I didn't want to do this again

But you hurt me so bad baby

I just want the pain to end

I know this hurts you

I feel so bad

I care for you more than myself

It's truly sad

No explanation

It's the same issues

Your sad heart hurts me

I'm just so sorry

What's Greater Part 1

What's greater

Your hate for me

Or your love that's unseen

Do you pray for me?

Send good vibes and high fives,

Lifting me up

Or will your strong hands give me a slap to my face

Does your word matter more than mine?

Because if it's not good in your eyes

Then it's a waste of your time

Will you ever be ok?

No matter how hard I try to cheer you up

It'll never be enough

And I'll have to hear you say

I wish you'd try

How can you not see me reaching for the sky?

There's no limit, to me

But in your eyes,

You lack, and you'll never be

Enough

And I've had it

I'm sick of you wishing on stars,

Hoping that you'll go far

You can't choose the days you work hard

Because life shows no mercy

And it'll forever be against you

You're so hyped up about your followers

And forget I'm down for you too

Even though my purpose in life is bigger than you

I still choose you

Yes, I'm still a fool

But have you ever been crazy about me?

Get out of your own head and help someone else

succeed

Not by bringing them down

Or dragging their confidence through the ground

And even after all that I still stuck around

I'm waiting on you to make a move

It's your turn to flip my frown upside down

January 21st, 2019

Cry for Help Part 1

I'm always trying to keep my name low

I could never stay faithful

Not to anyone or myself

I try to pray to God for help

But is it my fault that I don't surrender

Am I weak when I feel strong?

Defeating my confidence within this mindset

I wish all my feelings got along

Tears crowding my eyes, I can't see pass them

But I can see behind them

I stay stuck in the past because the

Present time never lasts

Even when I try to appreciate

The things at stake

I am not awake

I act like I have all day

I don't want to take 10 years rebuilding my face

I need help

I was never able to use my voice

I grew in fear

Even after all these years

I still never learned

Habits since my childhood never broke

Every step I take feels like I'm gonna get choked

With reality

And I still can't see

Who am I even supposed to be?

Do people like to be around me

Insanity consuming me

But just enough peace to get me by

What if I already wasted too much time

I'm not sure how to ask for help

So, I'm begging, please hear me now

Take me to a place where I do more than frown

Preferably my childhood when everything was great

Don't say that was a lie, it's the only thing I have left

that didn't break

Let's not say too much about my heart

There was one guy who tore that whole thing apart

Simply left me to die, but I'm still alive

And all those tears I cried helped me grow wings so I

could fly

And I still need help because I'm not perfect

And I never want to be

It's my time to shine but it'll take time

I need to start taking back what's mine

And have peace

Oh, how I miss having peace

My scars are healing so I can appreciate peace

My head is spinning so I can appreciate peace

Friends turned on me so I can appreciate peace

My whole world fell apart so I could appreciate peace

I'm thankful for what God gave me

Especially peace

But I don't always use His gifts

They're hidden underneath

No longer blinded, now I see

But I still need help

I need to help me be me

him.

Insanity driving me off the edge of my being

Shame was the shirt I put on, and it stuck to me

Agonizing every corner of my mind

Inner turmoil boiling up inside

Ache after heart ache, hoping to not wake

Hell was the name of your sanctuary

Wanting to gain enough strength to not return there

Everyday praying for a miracle

But never able to get over myself

Bothered internally by your darkness, until I come to

the light

his-story

You were my safe place
But filled with so much hate
You always hid your face
Tried your best to push me away
While hoping I would stay
How much dirt could I take

Show the real you, or remain fake
I thought this life was my fate
But I was wrong...
You emptied me 'til my love was gone
Waiting for you to love me when your hate was
strong
Crying on the floor, writing song after song

You never let me sing to you
My feelings were a symphony

Different notes scattered on the page waiting to attack me

I thought if you understood my pain then I would be freed

I thought if you recognized my shame, then you d give me what I need

I placed my heart in your hands and you dropped it
That night I told you no, you didn't stop it
I tried to push you off, but your mind was tricked
I was too shocked to scream, or even use my fists
Forced me to surrender, why have you done this

Regretting those nights I let you have your way with me

When I wasn't ok

Being manipulated into believing it s ok to love this way

Trying to break away
You forced me to remain
You said that you would change
I hope you'd change your name

At the end of the day, you let me carry all this shame

Alone

I tried to be fine even after the fact

I didn't report you, because I had your back

Your freedom was important to me, because you are

young and black

Yet you still shushed me

And you called me fat

How did I ever stay with someone who would do me

like that

You said you were nothing without me

I bleed, you bleed, we were a team

You threatened your life if I would ever leave

I stayed with you, I thought I was what you would

need

You rarely gave back to me, what a scheme

When I made efforts to be healthy, your toxicity

would intervene

Although you fascinated me with your wit and your

skills

It took forever for you to get a job
And you still barely paid any bills
I let so many things go, I let you do what you will
After all this, I was the one who was spiritually killed

But I always saw the good in you
I encouraged you to do better
You never told me what my faults were
You hid it underneath your sweater
When the old me cried out to you,
You wouldn't go get her
You left her

Secretly unpleased with things I would do
You never actually let your feelings show through
"Please don't get on my nerves today"
 Please don t be you"
But you told me I was your boo
So I thought our love was true

All this time I thought I was loving you the right way
Extra hugs, kisses, and food in your belly at the end
of the day

I carried this heavy burden alone like a slave
I checked on you often to see if you were ok
You rarely cared about where I was,
Or where I would stay

I disappointed you when I would never fit in your box
of ideal perfection
You thought I was your blessing, when I was really a
lesson
All the places I took you, all those things I taught you,
Did you ever really learn
Why did it take years for it to show?
You never earned my loyalty
Now I know

I did my dirt, I lied, I cheated, I treated you bad
But can that compare to how you treated me
Does this make you mad?
Go ahead and tell the world how you were perfect
and never did me dirty
Keep in mind all the things you did,
and that the love you gave was never worthy

I understand I drug your heart through the dirt

all that back and forth really made your heart hurt

But after that night, you became a different man

Please tell me why you stopped holding my hand

But then again...

We really hurt each other, and it was toxic

But you never really showed love, you left me in a pit

You started changing when it was too late

But I couldn't stay with you,

since you were the reason for the rape

Thinking on the things we use to get into

That we no longer do

Sends a shock to my system

And I'm not sure how I'll get ahead

I'm laying here hanging by a thread

On my bed, holding on for dear life

This is one of the worse kinds of fights

Feels like I'm losing

You have a new girl and no longer choosing

Me

I'm still a fool, you see!

But why take her to the places we use to be

It's sickening

I'm only happy for you because she keeps you from

me

But I'm sorry!

I can't help it!

Thinking on the old us

Puts me on the verge of an inner self destruction

My heart feels like It'll bust

Fighting all alone in the ring

I'm acting like you're my everything,

And feeling like I'm nothing

I saw you with her today, and I thank God that you

are

I pray with everything in me that in life you go far

As long as she keeps you out of my arms

I pray that one day I won't be blinded

By your looks and your charm

Lately I've been desperate for change

I no longer want to stay the same

I went through my process,

No longer using pain as a cane

It is true, without Jesus I am nothing

But I m everything with Him, in His name

Jesus, who is the living water calmed my soul

5 years later I had to escape from the things of old

Because I fear the one who can cast me away

By His grace He stayed, and His mercy didn't fade

I am now walking in the presence of God s glory

This was my past life, and this was his story

Selfish Stupidity

I give, you give
You take, I take
Everything was once ok
You began the race
And at a time it seemed like we d never stop running
Although insulting me in front of my face
You thought your deed was loving
Where did you think this would lead?
That one act made us both bleed
The wrong choice at the wrong time
I saw you wanted me to be fine
But your mind was tricked
After I told you, you couldn't do this
Reverse psychology for your reaction
Puffing yourself up, blasting
I m sorry I did that to you
For me this was brand new
I wish I could undo what we went through
But I blame my selfish stupidity too

I'll Be Better

I'll be better
No matter the day
No matter the weather
I'll be greater
No matter what it looks like
I don't care about haters
My circle is small
But I'll still get there
I'll keep standing tall
I'll force life to be fair
I'll be better
Only for myself
I'll see the light, I will be helped
I won't stay low for long
I'll keep writing more songs
I'll keep taking more steps
Until I have none left
Until I take my last breath

I'll crawl if I have to

I'll cry if I have to

I'll take bruises too

I'll try until my face turns blue

I will get better, and I'll do it for you

Dear, My Love

No more hi's, no more goodbyes
No more tears left to cry
And no more hugs
I gave you all my love, but you never used it
Instead, you wasted my time, and abused it
Dear my love, out with the old and in with the better
It's such a shame you never got it together
A little progress here and there
but not enough to make it fair
Not enough to pay back every dime
Not enough to replace the wasted time
Not enough to bottle all my tears
Even though I got love for you baby
It's a new year
Same me, different routine
Same me, but my soul has been cleaned
I wish you well, and be careful with your tainted soul
One broken heart should be enough

Turn that lesson you learned into pure gold

Aren't you glad you didn't dim my light?

Aren't you glad I can still shine bright?

Without you
Dear my love, you caused me to lose my mind

But God gave me a new one, and I'm doing just fine

So, don't worry about me

And don't worry about if I think about you

Because you know I am

I am much better off without you

Wet Lashes

Staring at my wet lashes in the mirror

I see a fighter

I'm just hoping my family was right about her

In my poem I said tears were crowding my eyes and I

couldn't see past them

I never imagined they'd fall down to my dress hem

This feeling honestly disgusts me

Nothing but tears and snot on my white tee

Feeling defeated after being set free

Attempting to live off prayers and herbal tea

I'm not enough for myself,

So, I seek my Lord

But when it gets heavy, I don't seek Him

I'm crying on the floor

He is the lifter of heads, He restores my soul

Thanks to me, I constantly run back to the things of

old

Don't confuse this with depression

This is just a beautiful lesson

To still be alive, and with God I thrive

But right now, in this moment,

I'm struggling to survive

Telling myself I'll be ok

Isn't that what a counselor would say?

Fruit snacks and juice for breakfast

I hate sitting in this when the pain hits

A pool of my tears is where I'll take a dip

I still value my life, don't get me wrong

I'll take more steps, I'll write more songs

I will get there

Just not today

In this pain, temporarily

Is where I'll stay

Sickening

Wanting to dive deeper into the depths of the
unknown
What if the real me was left there and I'm trying to
get her back
I recognized her by her scars that were never shown
Just like her heart and her skin, those scars turned
black
What if I don't know who I am now
Take me back to that place that scarred my soul
That place that has nothing but my tears on the
ground
And maybe it'll make me feel whole
All this time searching for healing within you,
When you couldn't even do it for you
I was dangerously in love
When I should've been looking for healing above
Wondering why I keep letting the one who forced
entry,
to reenter me

Going out of my way to let you in

I'm as obsessed as can be...

It's that same bed and those same strokes

That same cry, that same poke

That same yes, and that same no

Why couldn't I just let you go...

Maybe I wanted to be destroyed

Looking at your satisfied face while I crumble

into pebbles of shame

Maybe I want to be here

Misery absolutely loves company

Pretending to be fine just to avoid your broken face

Sparing you the horrifying details

Because your life is already so horrible

And you take it out on me

But I am your savior

And I fool myself everyday

If someone stabbed you, you wouldn't let them stab

you again with a prettier knife

Healthy desires fulfilled in filthy ways

I lay down in peace and arise with a mask of shame

There was never a named perpetrator,

But I knew you

I wouldn't allow you to go through what they went through

Take that rubber hook off your lip, it's no longer yours

But what I'll gladly leave you is my bleeding heart

Remember my face of shame, and that report that has no name

People aren't looking at you, they aren't looking for you

But they can see me clearly

It's my blood that's splattered all over me,

Not yours, because you broke me

You didn't bother to try to fix me

Left me with broken pieces and slurred speeches

To figure out why I lost my ability to shout

But you shushed me, you put your hands on me

You held me down and smiled at me

You're the one who never heard my cries

I wondered why I thought you would hear them now

I wondered why I thought you had the key to those loose chains I held onto

I was your fool, but I wondered why you always had to be so cruel

Thanks to you my thoughts are bickering

These memories are sickening

September 3rd, 2020

Growing a Heart of Repentance

Look in my eyes
And you'll see I'm broke down, busted, and
disgusted
I hate my room, walls, and my small bed
The struggle is so real, trying to get these thoughts
out of my head
I know I'm wrong, I know I'm dead
But it feels so good giving in
How do I explain this?
Where do I begin...
It started even when I was under the age of 10
Almost didn't care about how, where, or when
Long days grew to dark nights
I was too young to understand I had to fight
All I knew was that it felt right
But don't let anyone know, stay out of sight
God says if you don't stop, you won't be my friend

God wants to use me, He said I have an expected end
Sin could never inherit the kingdom
But once again, Lord, I'm looking for freedom
Try me again!
Help me fight this war that's within
You said blot my eye out if it causes me to sin
But every now and again I get it together
Only by Your grace until the next stormy weather
Until the next snowstorm
And I only do it to get warm
But that little spark turned into a flame
And that one thought quickly turned into shame
I don't know my name, because I'm high right now
Masking the pain, not caring if I die in this house
My flesh rises up like a tsunami
Sin folding my spirit like origami
I'm broken
I can hold off until my trigger words are spoken
I need this
I need this to love me back
I give it so much attention without slack
All I get in return is a slap,

in my feelings

Inching closer and closer to the edge of the cliff

Because I told myself if I don't stop that this is it

My life slipping away from me slowly

When all God wanted was for me to be lowly

To surrender to Him

But I'm working hard through my process

You give me the strength to say no

Those days I lazily pray to You,

That's when my true feelings show

It gets harder to suppress

And easier to express the wickedness of my own heart

Teach me to love what You love

And hate what You hate, is what I should pray

Consistency with You will make me stay

But I continue to fade away

My flesh is never ok

But You made this day, You created me out of clay

For we know that the law is spiritual,

but I am carnal, sold under sin

The good I want to do, I don't

And the wrong that I hate, I do it again

My war is within

Father God, I know You heareth not sinners

But please give me another chance

You already won, so I'm a winner

Still, don't let me slip into a trance

You woke me on this day

So, I know Your forgiveness is possible

Don't take Your spirit away just yet Lord

With The Holy Spirit I can be unstoppable

I can't live this life without You

I breathe because You allow it

Lord, help me please, don't let me die in this pit

Yes, my heart is deceitful above all things,

And my own lusts put me here

But You Lord search the heart,

You try the reins

Lord You re the one who told me not to fear

Lord, You re the one who can set my soul free

When you set me free, I will be free indeed

So I will look to the hills from whence cometh my
Help

And I will receive Your help

Once I come out of self

What's Greater Part 2

What's greater
My love for you,
Or my ambition to get through
You see, I prayed for you
But you're so wrapped up in your new girl you'll
never notice what my prayers do
All those years I sent you good vibes and lifted your
head high
when you could barely hold it yourself
You don't remember that you always asked for my
help?
But what did I get in return,
Your love?
Your poisonous, selfish, toxic love
That was obviously never sent from above
Yes, we had our good times, and we had some really
great sex
But, excuse me mister, you certainly were not the
best

I had my flaws too, but which one of us ALWAYS came through?

No, I wasn't everything you needed when you needed it

But you said it yourself, we were a perfect fit!

You gave 20, and I gave 80

Yeah, we were still 100, but your love was shady

Yes, your love was shaky

One minute you'll cry if I leave, and the next you hate me

After a while, you weren't ok with me

Not while I was blazing through the city at the times you couldn't see

Me

Could you ever see me?

Or the person you wanted me to be?

Be honest, you were in love with being in love

On the same hand, I was the same

I was in love with the old you, and after a while you had changed

All I wanted was for you to hold my hand

Why did you make me ask for that again and again?

You wondered why I couldn't fit in your box of ideal

perfection

I wondered why you could never take correction

Don't call your girl names, be respectful, don't be a

fool

Kicking me while I was down and needed you, that

wasn't cool

Let me tell you what I think is cool,

This breath I breathe without you

Because going back to you is something I will not do

What's greater is my new heart that God gave me

Yeah, some days are shaky,

But no one can tell me I won't make it

I'm now strong enough to not stick around

Even after those times I saw you in town

You don't have to put a smile on my face,

I smile anyway

I just remind myself that I no longer need you to

brighten up my day

I know you don't care about me,

but I still hope you're ok

Be ok, while my love for you fades away

Cry for Help Part 2

I try to keep my name low to lift His name high
The Lord made my spirit glow, and that's the part
that needs to show,
Because it's not about you or I
I started taking the Lord with me everywhere, and
guess what?
Life became fair
I know where the real battle is
We war in our minds
I use God's word as my armor,
I consult the one who sits outside of time
God humbled me to the passenger's side so He
could drive
I look in my rearview to appreciate the things you
allow to fall by
Jesus Christ rose my soul that was once dead
I am risen with Him, that's what I said
It's not time to sleep, so get out of bed

The bible says if you love slumber, you'll lose your bread

You'll lose that dough

The cash won't flow

Your soul will hang low

But don't allow me to tell you I told you so

For the love of money is the root of all evil

It'll make your faith drop

Picking up God's word will help you mount up with wings like eagles

All eyes on God, you'll soar to the top

Don't side with the world to upgrade your story

Your body is a living temple,

Use it for God's glory

Playing with God you'll lose your place in this race

Throw away shame, rid the blues

It's best to keep that same face

Be real. Be honest. Be true.

The abundant life can be for you too

You just have to choose

God says, it's either Me or you

This cry for help is not for me, my help comes from the Lord

*But this war cry is for you, recognize who you're
fighting for*

*Don't worry about anything, because He provides
opens doors*

*The ones He closed are for your good, you shouldn't
ask for nothing more*

Come as you are, He'll change you for the better

You'll be able to stand tall through any weather

The law of the Lord is perfect, converting the soul

Seek God now, and He'll make you whole

Healed

Am I healed or am I still healing?

There's an ache when I let go of those dangerous

inner feelings

But oh, what a joy it is to be free

We had to get rid of the old me

Now The LORD is that spirit, and Where The Spirit of

The LORD is, there's freedom

I'm just glad I came to my senses and realized I need

Him

No longer hurting in silence

Every day, this pain fades away

Not resulting to violence

When He arrives, He wants to stay

I had to open my heart and my mind

Living without Him had me feeling like I was out of

time

It felt like the end for me

Waking up in darkness, I could barely see

It felt like that was it, no more sanity

But He healed me

My God healed me

Oh, what a joy it is to be free

It's not something you can buy or earn

In a lifetime, these lessons could never be learned

On your own

My God is greater than anything you were ever

shown

The invisible God forever reigns on high

Being free in Him means I can fly

I wouldn't trade this healing for anything in the

universe

I'm just thankful to God that He gave me a new life in

exchange for my hurt

To be healed is like resting in a flow of living water

I'm so thankful that God calls me His daughter

Fight Ready

The whole squad is out here with a child
But I'm not really hanging with that crowd
I'd rather be focused on the Lord
Don't you hear Him knocking on the door
Of your heart
Give Him the whole thing
Aren't you tired of fighting all alone in that ring?
Gloves on, mouthguard in, but only fighting with
yourself
For once try being humble, it's ok to ask for help
Everybody knows that you were hurt, because you
act it out
You put that smile on your face when you really
wanna shout
You just got corrected and now you wanna pout
Don't hold onto that negativity, just throw it out
Why do I have to rhyme through my lines to make
you see what I'm talking about?
Oh, you have questions?

All answers are in the Lord!

He should be the only one you're fighting for

Never give up, and don't give in

When you're team Jesus, He said you'll always win

I'll say again, give Him your whole heart

He'll fix your life up that you thought fell apart

You need rest? Get it from the best!

And thank God for life, that your heart is beating in your chest

If you're racing in your mind, He'll surely give you peace

Always remember Isaiah 26:3

You can stay woke, and also catch some Z's

Don't let no one think you're crazy for getting what you need

And if they try to curse you, remember Matthew 5:44

God says we need to pray for our enemies

God is the one we do that for

Have no fear, because the Lord is still here!

Anyone who's willing, with an ear, let him hear

The Almighty God is speaking, you just have to draw near

Cast all your cares upon Him, because He cares

Remember everywhere you go, He is there

So stop fighting with yourself, stop pushing God away

I'm trying to tell you, it's better for you to get saved

Jesus is our hero, and He's saving everyday

Give your all to God and acknowledge Him in every way

And trust me when I say, that if you don't give up, you're going to be ok!

My LORD

Thank You LORD for being the lighthouse in the

center of my storm

You Lord are the sun in darkness

Your victory became mine when the veil was torn

Of Your Holy Spirit, I will be cautious

You were my voice when I didn't know how to use my

own

You placed melodies within me, You re amazing, my

mind is blown

You are my God, You are my King

You defended my purpose like young David with the

sling

You are the song on my tongue that brings joy to my

heart

Oh, how You hold me when I break so I don't fall

apart

Thank You for always being with me at night when I

felt alone

Most High, You are my strength, my strong tower, my

stone

All my tears I cried You bottled them up

No one else's love was ever enough

Your grace overflows, when You fill my cup

You re always on time, even when the going gets

tough

I wanted to fall but You wouldn't let me

I almost fell but that wasn't meant for me

I was once blinded, but now I can see

The love You have for me, no other can compete

The Way You Love Me

Careful when you fall, so you don't get scraped

Walking down patiently so our love doesn't turn into
hate

One and one

Keeping the same pace

Two plus three, together running the race

With God, you, and me, our circle is complete

Did I mention I love how you love me?

You always seek guidance from above

Let our purity continue to fly high, like a dove

When I go too fast you slow me down

You laugh with me when I act like a clown

Our God still provides when things get tight

If we ever go left, He makes us right

You keep me cool when the flame gets too hot

I feel safe with you, rather you're here with me or not

It's the way you tell me to calm down when I'm
freaking out

And the way you pray for me when I'm feeling doubt

It's the way we lift His name together

Keeping the faith through any weather,

Let's me know we can make it

We're honest with each other, we don't have to fake

it

If God leads the way, I know we'll be ok

Even if I have to be without you for a day

I hope you stay by my side

Because for the first time, I have nothing to hide

As much as I can give, my love is yours to keep

So take your time and walk slow, the steps are steep

It's a long way down, because my love is deep

I just thank God that you love me for me

My Love

Soaking within God s glory
Never afraid of what goes before me
Privileged to experience our Lord in this way
Lord, keep us in Your presence forever, please stay
You gave us permission to love this way
You showed us the real meaning of love
Daily seeking out our flesh to slay
We want to be the ones You are proud of
And it s ok, that we might not always see the best of
days
But there will never be a dull one
Why?
Because the veil was torn when the Son was hung
You ordained this love, only You did it, because
You re able
When counterfeits tried to join in, You removed them
from the table
The Father, the Son, the Holy Ghost, and I
Faith, prayer, The Word, and my guy

Together we will thrive

It s a team effort

Thanking You Lord that we've made it out alive

You Lord have always made streams in the dessert

What I have now was definitely worth the wait

This love is worth the hurt

Lord we know You never make mistakes

You dried the tears that fell on my shirt

I understand now why any other guy and I would split

Their heart was the wrong size, we didn't fit

Lord You helped me let go of me, and You sent him

Lord, You dwell inside us, true love from within

A man who puts You first, and waits for Your instruction

We let go of our old ways that led to an inner self destruction

Not interested in wasting time, because we know You're on Your way

Have Your way in us and through us, every time, everyday

Lord, allow this love to bring glory to Your name

Thank You for Your faithfulness, and we'll be careful to do the same

November 30th, 2020

New Me

2020, new vision

Walking into my new beginning

Shedding off the old Bre

Because it was only ever meant to help me

When I look in the mirror, I want to see someone

worthy of love

All that I endured surprisingly gave me a shove

I needed that push

I needed to fall on my tush

I bumped my head quite a lot

But I finally learned my lesson, soon, I forgot

I had lost my way, crawling my way to The Sun

But God taught me how to run

To a place to be forgiven for all the wrong I've done

Pay more attention to the new song I've sung

If there's any good in me, it's not me, it's God

He rose just so I could choose

He gave me a million tries so I could never lose

Found my voice and took it back

Never again to be a toy, to be used and abused

Never again letting my scars turn black

In my past life I was never amused

Living for the moment, letting time slip by

I look back now, and I understand why

I know why my struggle was so hard

I was the one who caused my own scars

Constantly stuck, going nowhere fast

I couldn't realize why the bliss didn't last

But things changed for me

And I thank God for healing

No longer led by my feelings

Let the emotions fall away

Super thankful to The LORD that He stayed

Thank You LORD for dying on that tree

LORD, it'll forever be You and me

My LORD taught me how to Be Ready Everyday And Never Afraid

For this truly is the day that The LORD has made

About the Author

Breana Smith is a young lady who lives in Philadelphia, Pennsylvania with her mom and two cats. As a child, she began writing song lyrics, with dreams of one day becoming a Rockstar and a lyricist. As Breana grew older, she discovered her love for poetry through a means of expressing feelings during the toughest parts of her life. One of those tough seasons was in 2020 during the coronavirus pandemic, when The LORD set her totally free from the pain of her past, despite the chaos. She is a firm believer in The Gospel of Jesus Christ and considers herself a follower of Jesus' teachings. Breana discovered that God called her to use her voice to help others and to advance His kingdom. Today, she works a full-time job, and mentors three teenagers she calls family through bible studies. Breana believes that poetry is a great way to create art, express emotions, and tell stories. It is her goal to use the poetic gift that God gave her to communicate to the youth that they are not alone in their struggles. She wants them to come to know Jesus Christ for themselves and be released from all kinds of bondage so they can live an abundant life through Christ. Breana believes that with Jesus, anything is possible! If He can change her life for the better, He can do it for anyone!

* 9 7 8 0 5 7 8 8 4 6 0 6 4 *